Letters to My Grandchildren

My Advice for a Happy Marriage

By George Richard Seddon, Sr.

Letter Number One

Dear Grandchildren,

*I*t is highly unlikely that I will be able to speak to each of you individually about the subject of marriage. So, I have decided to speak through a series of short, easy to understand letters. Except for this letter, the numbers assigned do not necessarily rank the importance that I believe each subject deserves.

This first letter is an exception because the subject is vastly more important to you as an individual than just to marriage.

Above all else that you do, it is vitally important that you accept Jesus Christ as your personal Savior! Once you've accepted Jesus you must have a continuing, daily, personal relationship with Him. I am not talking about church denomination or any other related subject. The critical, vastly important question is: Have you surrendered your life to Christ? If not, **do it now, right now** without delay.

I am certain, from personal experience, that the quicker you make a public profession of your faith, the better. Remember, and never forget, that success is simply getting up one more time than you fall. Jesus himself tells us that if we confess our sins he is faithful and just to forgive us! You can believe this. It is true!

In closing this first letter I must tell you in no uncertain terms that you, as a believer, should **only** date, fall in love with, and marry another born-again believer. I mean someone completely dedicated to the Christian faith.

If I am available it would give me the greatest joy possible to share with you verbally the importance of this subject. I would like to share living experiences that support my convictions. After 58 years of wonderful life with the greatest wife on earth, we're no longer novices about this subject.

With all my love,
Grandfather

Letter Number Two

Dear Grandchildren,

Since you are my grandchildren, I know you have been to church. This letter is about much more than attending church. Obviously, I think you should attend church faithfully, as often as you have opportunity! But again this letter only starts with the assumption that you are attending a church.

I am fully persuaded that you as a believer should do more, **much more**, than simply attend. The body of Christ is alive and needs you in your place of service to function properly.

Finding your place in the local body of believers is of critical importance. Just think of your *personal body for a second. You will realize that you don't have any unimportant body parts. The very same thing holds true with the body of Christ. Every individual person is important.*

Every church, including the one I presently attend, has more opportunities to serve than there are people wanting to serve. This should not be! I am personally persuaded that unless you are directed by the Lord himself you should meet with the pastor in charge of your age group. You should share with the pastor your skills, talents, and most of all your desire to serve the body of Christ in the church.

Often there will be areas of service where both husband and wife can serve as a team. These include the choir, orchestra, a Sunday school class, or greeters at the doors of the church, just to name a few. Also remember and never forget that no one job is forever. As your skill, talent, and abilities grow, so will your responsibility to the body.

In closing, it is important for you to never forget that the body of Christ only needs your service two times. <u>First,</u> every time you feel like serving, and <u>second,</u> when you don't feel like serving.

With all my love,
Grandfather

Letter Number Three

Dear Grandchildren,

*I*f you are old enough to be reading this letter by yourself, you are, or will sometime in the future be considering marriage. Wow, what a thought! I can still remember the first time I thought about getting married.

Let me begin by telling you that I grew up without grandparents. My mother and father were married to each other for their lifetime. The first 18 years of my life was lived in their home. All I learned about the subject of marriage was from them.

Now, after 58 years of married life with the most wonderful wife, mother, grandmother, great grandmother, sweetheart, and a host of additional love names all wrapped up in one beautiful package (your grandmother, Baby Bob) I will boldly give you the following advice.

Your wedding day can be the starting point of a truly great marriage! It all depends on the two of you. Note that the last three words of the previous sentence were plural and singular.

You and you alone will determine if you have a "ho-hum, just get by, miserable, dreary, kind of marriage". Look around and you can find plenty of them. Or, you can have a "super exciting, every growing, wonderful life" for as long as you both shall live. It is up to you!

Of course, you will have to work together. Sometimes it will be hard work. Sometimes it may be <u>very</u> hard work. When two lives that have been lived as individuals become "one life" there will always be some kind of work to be done. It's a dumb person who becomes an adult and stops! My grandchildren are very smart because Grandma says so!

Mr., learn what makes your wife happy and then do it! Mrs., discover what your husband likes and do it! I'm not talking about sex, that's another letter. Just make sure that you enjoy being together more than whatever else you may be doing. This doesn't happen overnight. In the process of growing together you will both experience new, first-time for you, experiences. That's great.

The important thing is to grow together! You both must continue to grow individually, but when you are married, enjoy growing towards each other by doing new things that perhaps neither of you has ever done before. This might be hot air ballooning, parasailing, or floating down the river in a flatboat. It's not nearly as important what you do as the fact that you do it together. Remember and don't ever forget, anyone can marry and grow apart. A lot of couples do that without even trying. That's the problem. They don't work at their marriage until they are equally happy.

Did I mention that my grand children are very smart? Grandma says so!

With all my love,
Grandfather

Letter Number Four

Dear Grandchildren,

When I was a young person, many years ago, if someone asked about a Bible they were thinking of the King James Version. Why, you might ask? It was because the KJV was the only one available to the English speaking people. Other languages had Bibles which were printed just for them. Today this is not so. Your grandmother and I have close to 40 Bible for the two of us. As I write this letter I have beside me one Bible containing four popular translations in parallel columns. The King James Version, Modern Language, Living Bible and the Revised Standard Version.

However, my intent for this letter is not to discuss translations, but something far more important. Having time to read the Bible and pray together. Let me start by telling you that of all the many, many adjustments each of you will make, this area will be one of the most difficult and at the same time one of the most important.

Contrary to some people's opinion, we are created equal! We all receive the exact same amount of time. Down to the last second. The difference comes in what we do with what we have. Couples that read the Word together and pray together, stay together.

I am personally persuaded that one of the duties of men (husbands) is to take the lead in this area. Failure to build a strong spiritual life is to ignore one third of your being. Two thirds of a life will never be a successful life no matter how many other things we acquire. I am sure that couples who are too busy to pray together and read together are too busy!

In our married life we have acquired many, many books to help us understand the Bible. Let me encourage you to use whatever helps you as long as they strengthen your determination to read the Bible and pray together.

Your grandmother likes to sit in a bath tub full of hot water (hot water that could cook a lobster)! So one year, probably more than 20 years ago, we decided to read the entire Bible out loud with her sitting in the tub and me sitting on the floor. We used a Bible divided into 365 days. Each day we would read portions of Scripture from the Old Testament, New Testament and the Psalms.

Obviously, the better you know the author of the Bible, not just the men who used the pen, the more the Bible will mean to you. Always remember and never forget couples that read together and pray together, stay together.

With all my love,
Grandfather

Letter Number Five

Dear Grandchildren,

Before I was old enough to understand its meaning I heard adults say, "All work and no play makes George a very dull boy". While it's true I did not understand what they meant then, I certainly do now. This letter is **not** at all about work. It is about play.

Listen my grandchildren and I will tell you a story that is so sad but yet so true. I know, I really do, couples whose entire lives consist of working at a job, sleeping, eating together sometimes, working at everything, maybe having sex occasionally, and always wondering if this is what marriage is all about. I'm sure you will agree that is sad. But it does not have to be in your marriage. It is up to both of you.

You can and you should and we hope you will make playtime a priority for both of you together. Please note that I used the word together. Yes, it is nearly as sad to say that we also know marriages where one partner plays and the other works. Sometimes I think this is even worse.

We define playtime as anything and everything that you can learn to enjoy together. Some couples enjoy doing certain activities together and think of it as play, while other couples would consider the same activity work. Is planting a garden work? Well, it depends on who you ask and what they're enjoyment is.

The important thing is not what you do, but that you learn to enjoy it together. Your grandmother and I came from totally different backgrounds. We could not have been more different and still be from the same planet. But over the past 58 years it is hard, really hard, to imagine how many different activities we have enjoyed together. No, we're not joined at the hips. We truly, truly, like each other in addition to being in love.

Playtime does not equal money time. Table games at home with children and perhaps other couples and their children can provide an enjoyable playtime. You can add hot dogs, chips, and ice tea to the fun. Playtime can be riding bicycles acquired at yard sales, wearing helmets of course. Have fun with homemade washer boards that all ages can play. The list goes on and on. You will quickly discover that playtime never arrives by accident.

Always remember and never forget, people who say we will have playtime sometime, never do because sometime is never now.

With all my love,
Grandfather

Letter Number Six

Dear Grandchildren,

Many years ago a short story floated around as someone's attempt at humor. It went something like this. The wife says to her husband; "We've been married 20 years and you never told me that you love me." Her husband responds; "I told you that at the wedding. If I change my mind I'll tell you". I know you will agree with me that some people's humor is really sick.

Hopefully you were reading this before marriage or at least early in your marriage. Attention to this letter will pay tremendous dividends.

You both (husband and wife) should learn and practice for a lifetime how to express your gratitude to each other. Start out before marriage and do it, do it, do it, until it becomes a natural habit. Get used to saying things like, "Thank you", "Let me help", Sweetheart, "Honey" "You're beautiful" and "You're handsome". These expressions are not corny! They are not outdated! There are many other expressions that come to my mind but I'm sure you get the idea.

I may as well make a confession. When I am out and about if I hear a husband refer to his spouse with terms like "the old woman", "the old battle axe" "the hag back home" or similar disparaging words, I make a mental note to avoid that person in the future. If they will talk about their spouse like that, what would they say about someone they didn't care for?

You may say, "Grandfather, married couples don't talk like that now". You're right of course, and they are not very smart! But you must remember that you are my grandchildren and your grandmother continually tells me how very smart you are.

Always remember and never forget...don't ever be more courteous, thoughtful or kind to strangers than you are to your own spouse and children.

With all my love and prayers,
Grandfather

Letter Number Seven

Dear Grandchildren,

*I*n this letter I want to share three simple thoughts. Yes, you will recognize them as being just simple thoughts, but with profound and lasting benefits to your marriage.

If you are married or planning on getting married, you've had one or more dates. From that first date (if you continued to date) you've worked at your friendship with each other. When you observe some marriages the last thing that comes to mind is friendship. This ought not to be! Examine your thought life. Who do you want to be near? Who do you want to spend time with? If it is not your spouse and family then you need to change the way you think!

Of course, there will be times for other friends, for activities when you both don't participate, but I am talking about your state of mind. Any married person who thinks marriage provides bed room privileges, a joint tax return and little else is deluded in their thinking. Your spouse should be your best friend, and much, much more! Remember no one controls your mind but you.

Demonstrate to your spouse on a continuing basis just how much you love them. Verbalize it, write it, give gifts, do acts of kindness, share hugs and kisses, love pats and touching. If necessary (it needn't be) get a book of helps. I have one on my shelf entitled "400 Ways to Say I Love You". Personally I believe in love notes.

Dated, handwritten, signed, and placed where your spouse will easily find them. This has been going on in our life for 58 years so I can personally recommend it.

Here is a really heavy tip for a happy marriage. Always be quick to apologize! Your grandmother and I made a vow before we married that after we married we would never go to sleep at night until we could hug, kiss, and say "I love you". Sure, in the first few years there were times when we didn't sleep, we saw the sun come up, but neither of us would apologize. And then we remembered our vow! We both grew and developed even though we occasionally suffered from lack of sleep in those early years. Believe it or not, we still have to apologize but I can't remember when we last lost any sleep. Understand, God never intended for the two of you to be just alike (and you never will be) but over time, your lives will blend into one beautiful marriage. Always remember and never forget that an apology without sincerity is worse than no apology at all.

With all my love and prayers,
Grandfather

Letter Number Eight

Dear Grandchildren,

*T*o say the words "A person sees what they're looking at" seems so simple. But, let's think about it for a moment. It is also true that most of us find the things we look for. How does this work in marriage?

As each partner focuses on the positive qualities of their mate, the marriage continues to improve. I cannot begin to explain why human nature finds it easier to see negative things (faults) in their mate than to see positive attributes. I do know that God doesn't make junk. So, focus, focus, and focus some more on the positive qualities of your mate. It is so possible to develop negative thought patterns until we believe negative things are true whether they are or not.

You have heard the short rhyme that says, "There's so much bad in the best of us and so much good in the worst of us, it behooves all of us not to talk about the rest of us". It may seem a little silly at first but it points out the truth of what I'm trying to say.

You and you alone will determine how your mind works. With prayer and practice you can develop positive attitudes and learn to focus all of the positive attributes of your spouse. You can! You should! And, I believe you will.

Now this is a little different thought.

Never, and again I say never embarrass your mate in public. Start your marriage out by agreeing to never put each other down even in private conversations. First of all, private conversations are never as private as you might think! Second, if you don't allow the thought to stay in your mind it will never come out of your mouth. There will be times during group situations when it might see the fun thing to do. It is never fun. It is never the right or acceptable thing to do. One of the dumbest, completely dumb rhymes that you heard as a child says, "Sticks and stones may break my bones, but words will never hurt me!" That is a lie! Always remember and never forget, an audible word spoken can never be erased!

This letter is not intended to be a sermon but rather a couple of suggestions that will really enhance your marriage. You might have started out thinking your marriage was made in heaven! Who know, perhaps it was. But I am very sure, very sure that you will, like all others, live it out here on earth.

With all my love and prayers,
Grandfather

Letter Number Nine

Dear Grandchildren,

You have heard from someone, sometime, that grandfather graduated from Florida State University with a major in accounting and business. After graduation I became a certified public accountant and managed an accounting firm in Tallahassee for almost 40 years. If ever a man enjoyed his employment it was me. I had great clients, great employees, a terrific wife, and a super family. In my wildest imagination I could not have imagined being more blessed than this. Now I want to share a couple of tips that I probably first learned from my accounting clients.

It seems today couples go to great lengths planning their wedding. And from then on whatever happens, just happens. It is one way to live but in my humble opinion it is not the best way to live. It has been said that experience is the best teacher. I have discovered that by watching what others do and seeing the results of their actions is also a way to learn what to do and what not to do.

It seems today a lot of young couples make great plans for a beautiful wedding; they have the wedding and never plan anything else. I strongly recommend that you plan, plan, plan. Plan your work, plan your play, and plan your financial budget. Let me suggest that you jointly study finance until you have budgeting down to a fine art.

After preparing a budget live according to its dictates. Plan your days off from work, your vacations, and so much more. Have short term goals and long term goals of 3, 5, and 10 years. Of course, your plans will need adjusted from time to time and some of your early plans and goals may never be realized. With a plan you will at least have an idea of where you are going.

Plan your Christian service together and of course you should plan to give back to your community in some type of social service. Enough about plans!

In closing I suggest that you jointly realize that "All things are possible to them that believe", the Scripture says so! Once you are convinced of it, start living that way. Exciting things can and will happen.

With all my love and prayers,
Grandfather

Letter Number Ten

Dear Grandchildren,

We have seen multitudes of changes in technology during the last 58 years! One of the many changes has to do with digital video cameras. Wow, you can capture anything, anywhere, anytime and have it in a memory bank. We have a few paper pictures of our wedding and those present at that time. These are among our greatest treasures. We would encourage any couple getting married to record the event in every way possible.

If you were blessed to make these recordings, your assignment from this letter will be easier.

I truly believe that you both should review your commitment to each other often! Of course, anniversaries are a good time to review. Providing you celebrate anniversaries four or more times a year. I believe you should study the traditional marriage vows until you can quote them and understand them.

About 10 years ago we acquired a "Commitment Certificate". The actual name on the document is "Our Marriage Covenant". This document is approximately 24" wide and 18" high, printed in gold with spaces for husband and wife to sign along with lines for two witnesses. Our covenant was signed on November 27, 2001 and hangs on our bedroom wall. We read it out loud to each other on a regular basis.

Wedding pictures in an album, videos, certificates, and other memorabilia can be used to review your commitment to each other. Consider them as helps since what comes from your heart through your lips is the most important thing in your marriage.

It is easy to slip into the second suggestion. Communicate with each other. Talk about the weather, sports, sermons, but most of all have times when you talk heart to heart with each other. Talk together until you can read each other's mind more often than just at bedtime. Some of you will tell me your personality is just to be quiet. And I will respond by telling you that your body and lips will respond to whatever stimuli your mind commands.

Always remember, and never forget, smart couples that pray together and share together (verbally, physically, emotionally, and spiritually) stay together. And needless to say your grandmother reminds me often of how smart your all are.

With love and prayers,
Your Grandfather

Made in the USA
Middletown, DE
06 March 2015